Suspended in Emotion

Maya Weatherspoon

BookLeaf Publishing

Presentation by *BookLeaf Publishing*

Web: www.bookleafpub.com

E-mail: info@bookleafpub.com

ISBN: 9789357441254

First edition 2023

To Me. From Me.

ACKNOWLEDGEMENT

Life! I feel you constantly.

Thank you

PREFACE

When I am unable to express, I write.
Sometimes I try to write by reciting
the words over and over in my head.
Knowing that I will soon forget.
Many words have become etched in my heart,
lost in the labor of life.
No one really knows how poetic life is for me.
I can see both the beauty and the strife in most things.

After a very dark decade, I am learning to trust my words, and myself again.
So now I will begin to share Me.

Suspended in Emotion

I live my life suspended in emotion
constantly
hopelessly
trying to connect in my depth
encapsulated in the shallows
surrounded by impotence and
unsympathetic perception
so I subsist poignantly
Suspended in Emotion

The Tunnel to My Heart

I remember
searching for love
running so fast
that I could not see
I only paused to see
the way he looked at me
his eyes would
rest on my face
but was it my eyes he seeked
and if so;
could he see me
Before the answers would come
his eyes would escape
falling to
my lips
my tits
my thighs
and I learned
to think
that love
was in the lies
In cherishing
the lips
tits
and thighs

One by One
until they fell apart
and exposed
what he thought
was the tunnel
to my heart
it was warm and inviting
his touch excited me
my heart beat faster
racing toward
this love disaster
You could feel
my pulse inside
after the ride
our eyes met
we both
saw the lies
but he was
still there
between
my thighs
feeling
my heartbeat
in the tunnel
it was warm and inviting
but my soul
was cold
and retreating
so I closed my eyes

to shut out the lies
and find the love
inside of me
that he couldn't see
because instead of
pulling me in
He let my
lips
tits
and thighs
WIN

And So Did I....

I Remember Loving You

I remember loving you
when my teeth
were winter white
and my skin
still looked new

When days ran together
because
there were no responsibilities
between me and you
there was just time

I remember loving you
when I got the scar
on my right arm
the first blemish
that I remember
with you

Now life
has left me
slightly scarred
from keeping your seed
safe inside of me
and the glow of my early youth

continues to fade
unnoticeable and continuously
and I remember loving you just because

I remember loving you
without the scars of my heart
on my mind
from you hurting me
time after time

I remember loving you
for no reason
now
I remember them all

Because I've had to justify
every single one
day to day with you
has not been fun
you look at me
like a deteriorating possession
but you adore
that I bear your name

You want me to
love you
like I used to
But
you don't

love me the same
I remember loving you
all night long
but now
those days are long gone

You keep
focusing on
what used to be
not growing with me
getting to know me
currently, relevantly
my views on politics
and society
still only concerned
with being
inside of me
and you
call it
Love
stripping the life
out of me
looking for fulfillment
in an empty touch
that I use
to love so much
that has now
become a habit
a thoughtless act

repeated so many times
now
it just..... is

I remember loving you
for no reason at all
I just did....

It's Heavy

When you love someone who is growing and
learning
at the expense of your feelings and emotions;
it becomes so draining
At some point
understanding and patience
is irrelevant, a moot point
a juxtaposition
My Loyalty to self
is so much greater than my loyalty
to Anyone else

Morning Sex

It was a beautiful August Morning
The birds Chirping
The sun bright and warm
My skin was glowing
the sex we just had
also warming my complexion

His hands were reserved
but needy
he handled me with care
as though I would break
if he unleashed all of his passions at once
his stroke was a demand on my body to respond
and my every nerve stood at his attention
with the rhythm of my hips
as his guide
I became his.
And my pulsating punnani
throbbing to my heart song
reminds me of his rhythm
all day long

It was a beautiful August Morning
and it had just begun...

The Stranger who walks with me

My conscious mind is my friend;

my subconscious mind is the stranger

that teaches my friend Who I Am.

Between the Sheets

Every night
there were earthquakes
between the sheets
in my body
as our souls united
the pain
was washed away
by my climaxx
flesh to flesh
heart to heart
We betrayed all
except each other

Us

There was no need
to wipe away
the overflow
animalistic
was the desire
It was raw passion
finding its release
once again
in the arms
of each other
as we have done
so many
times before
then
we reached
simultaneously
wanting more
with eyes closed
the Chemistry
were intoxicating
I Love
This High
between us.

flying through ecstasy
holding on

for dear life
to my lover
for fear
that I might fall

Don't Ask

Just let me
in my way, in my time
because my mind
instantly feels overstimulated
by my emotions
and I can't find the words because
there are too many
it is not what I say
it is what I do
Listen with your heart
not your ears
love me with your actions
not your words
and just let me
in my way
in my time

Hear Me Scream

Writing allows me to scream in silence
It allows me to mask all of the
The hurt, disappointments, the pain
I am most verbal when
I'm Quiet

Today

You find yourself trying to forget
trying to block out the pain
then something comes along and derails you
a song
a scent
a sound
The crickets did it today

her

She yields herself
to the pleasures of her lover's desire
never limiting access to her feminine energy
she is welcoming and open to the tenderness
that exists when in love

Unfinished Business

It was an instant attraction
The moment their eyes met
She felt he was her forever
She moved on the promise of love she saw in his eyes

She longed for his touch
and to lay her head on his chest
to be enveloped in his masculinity
She wished to imagine her name in the rhythm
of his heartbeat
He was intoxicating and intense
his touch, his kiss, his gaze

all passion and intensity
he bombarded her
with attention
disarming her
with false admiration and lies
fake affection and care
in the silence
she remembered
his words
she remembered
the way he said her name and-

The Silent Treatment

Words are my most powerful weapon
in their absence
I am weak
I am vulnerable
I am in pain

Leather Rose

She wore pain like a diamond
it adorned every extremity
It added to her charm
She was fragrant and pretty
a manifestation of femininity
alluring and powerful
empathetic and compassionate
nurturing and supportive
passionate and submissive

and pain has given her thorns

Emotional Pain

It arrests a deep breath
quickens the heart
voids initiative
diminishes joy

to know it
is to remember it
is to avoid it
is to extinguish it
it to suppress it

a constant reminder
to not allow yourself
to feel
anything

In Vain

I tried desperately
to communicate the passion
that I felt
I used words that were misunderstood
I used touch that did not permeate
I used my presence that was taken for granted
I cried alone
screamed into my pillow
I waited;
in vain

Invisible

awakened to a new world
though nothing has changed
except me
my perspective
my feelings
difficult to explain
a feeling in relation to life
and your position in it
to be confined in discomfort
and your station, your penance
trapped in a life that is living you
instead of being in the life
you're living

Stronger

I don’t always share my thoughts and feelings
it would be selfish to require you to exist in
that place with me
so I deal with you lacking
empathy and sympathy
I simply cannot manage anything else
I don’t have the energy to focus
on how things should be when my reality
is killing me
my scars, my wounds are internal
but
I am learning to live again

When I forget that you're gone

It's moments like this when I miss you most
when there's rain and wind
and .....remember when?

but you weren't there, because you're not here;

it's when everyone's asleep and I'm awake
During the witching hours when there's not a
peep
or when I see someone that remembers me

it's moments like this when I miss you most
when there's rain and wind
and then the sun comes out again
that's always a moment

Hey! remember when?.....

but you weren't there because you're not here

it's moments like this that I miss you the most
when there's air to breathe,
and I breathe it in.
Then there're moments like these,

where I'm just
remembering when....

I miss you

Suspended in ecstasy

She had been taught to suppress her sexuality
when inside her passions were ever churning
she envisioned him above her
ravishing her body in a carnal way
his passion was encompassing,
hers powerful but submissive
as he fed her his energy
his kiss hypnotized her to follow his every
command
she was unyielding to his desire
thereby feeding hers
the air around them charged with illuminating
energy
they were engulfed in the flames of passion
lost in each other
he held her as though she was trying to escape
pulling her close
anchoring her so he could have his way
his dominion was deep
steady
neither fast or slow
hard or soft
somewhere between pleasure and pain
controlled and demanding
the contrast drove her wild

she held on kissing, biting, sucking
trying to contain the moans that escaped her
he studied her
deciphering the language her body spoke to him
controlling his seed
he laid trails of kisses down her
body finally sucking on her treasure
as he ripped away all of her inhibitions
making her his
she begged him for her release
he was slow and deliberate
teasing her sweet spot
she responded with intentional motion
driving him deeper
matching his rhythm
making it hard for him to maintain control
she needed him
craved him
there were no words
only sounds and gazes
the bond deepened
they would forever crave this connection
never allowing their passion to deplete

www.ingramcontent.com/pod-product-compliance
Lightning Source LLC
Chambersburg PA
CBHW051751130826
49812CB00033B/1097
* 9 7 8 9 3 5 7 4 4 1 2 5 4 *